T0193267

Letters
to my
Friends

Paul's Letters

Anna Dickson
Illustrated by: Rorie Scroggins

WestBow Press books may be ordered through booksellers or by contacting:

WestBow Press
A Division of Thomas Nelson & Zondervan
1663 Liberty Drive
Bloomington, IN 47403
www.westbowpress.com
844-714-3454

Because of the dynamic nature of the Internet, any web addresses or links contained in this book may have changed since publication and may no longer be valid. The views expressed in this work are solely those of the author and do not necessarily reflect the views of the publisher, and the publisher hereby disclaims any responsibility for them.

Interior Image Credit: Rorie Scroggins

ISBN: 979-8-3850-0907-7 (sc)
ISBN: 979-8-3850-0909-1 (hc)
ISBN: 979-8-3850-0908-4 (e)

Library of Congress Control Number: 2023918785

Print information available on the last page.

WestBow Press rev. date: 12/27/2023

Dedication

To JD, thank you for helping me get the words from my old notebook onto these pages.
The best partner, encourager, and dream reacher. I love you.

And to my girls, my inspiration for this project, this is my gift to you. May you treasure
God's Word and the comfort and hope it brings all the days of your lives.

Hey there,
my name's Paul.

And I know the
greatest story of all.

I used to not know it; in my heart or my mind.

 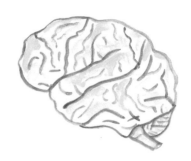

I couldn't even see it. In fact, I was blind.

But then I learned it:
the truth and the facts.

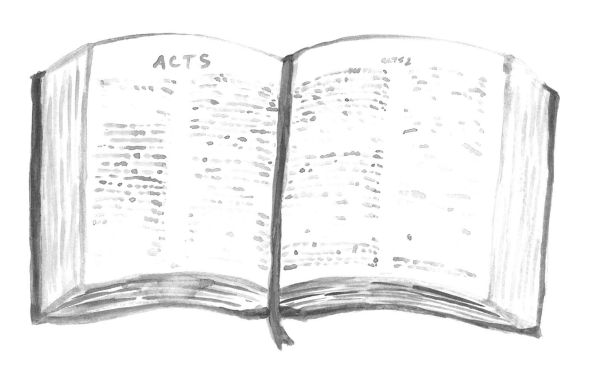

You can read about that
in a *book* called Acts.

But today's story is different.
I've got something to share.

They're letters I've written
to my friends everywhere.

To Jews and Gentiles, both friends of mine:
God's judgment and mercy are intertwined.

So, dear Romans, please be united as one.
Spread the Gospel and let bickering be done.

To my friends in Corinth –

First, please be humble,
don't try to compete.
Instead, share God's story to
build up the weak.

And second, you know
that I've had a hard time.
But my weakness is good.
It lets God's glory shine.

To those in Galatia, God's Spirit is near!
No longer in bondage, freedom is here!

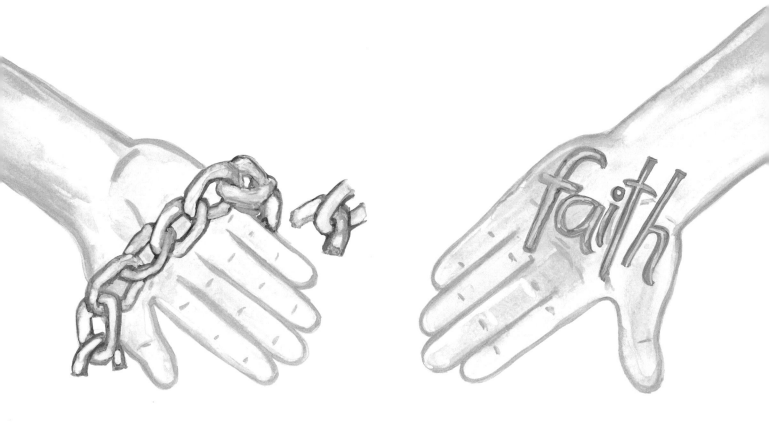

See, our Father will never be reached by law-keeping.
He came to us with the faith we are seeking.

To my friends in Ephesus –

Before God created,
He chose us to be His.

Adopted through Christ,
that's what Love is.

We were dead in our
sins, lost and alone.

But Christ made us
alive and brought
us all home.

To my dear Philippians,
in prison I sit.
You're doing so well.
Please do not quit.

You're serving your God
and each other, like Christ.

Jesus showed you how
by giving His life.

To the church in Colossae,
please do beware.
Run from false teachings,
but do not be scared.

Because Jesus is Lord over
all things, it's true.
O, He brought redemption
for me and for you.

To the Thessalonians, my new friends:
I want to assure you Christ will come again.

Out of death you will rise, praising His Name.
I'll write you again to tell you the same.

To my dear friend Timothy –
In Ephesus, thank you for staying behind.
In Jesus it's courage and strength that you'll find.

I'll write to you again, near the end of my days,
to ask for a visit and encourage you in your ways.

To Titus, my friend, thanks for staying in Crete.
You're helping the new churches know what to believe.

Because Knowing God affects how we behave,
so let's ask for help from the leaders God gave.

To Philemon, my friend, you have much to learn.
Forgiveness from friends should not be hard to earn.

The Gospel transforms how we treat one another.
No longer servants, we're sisters and brothers.

A letter to the Hebrews reads just like these:
hold fast to Christ, do not release.

There's no angel, no priest, no person who is better
than Jesus Christ for whom we write these letters.

So now it's your turn,
would you like to write?
Encouraging others is where
you'll set your sights.

Think of our God and His perfect Word, too.
Write letters to your friends,
and they may write to you.

Printed in the United States
by Baker & Taylor Publisher Services